Sharks

NATURE'S PREDATORS

Kris Hirschmann

KIDHAVEN PRESS

THOMSON
GALE

Detroit • New York • San Diego • San Francisco
Boston • New Haven, Conn. • Waterville, Maine
London • Munich

Picture Credits

Cover Photo: Chris Fallows/Apexpredators.com
© Tony Arruza/CORBIS, 40
© Tom Brakefield/CORBIS, 33
© Ralph A. Clevenger/CORBIS, 19
© Digital Stock, 9, 23 (bottom), 26
© Macdeff Everton/CORBIS, 41
Chris Fallows/Apexpredators.com, 4, 15, 25
© Bates Littlehales/CORBIS, 38 (bottom)
Minden Pictures, 30, 36, 38 (top)
© Amos Nachoum/CORBIS, 13
NOAA Photo Library, 35
Brandy Noon, 7, 8, 11, 18, 23 (top), 24, 39
© Jeffrey L. Rotman/CORBIS, 12, 20 (top, middle), 28
© Lawson Wood/CORBIS, 16, 20 (bottom)

Library of Congress Cataloging-in-Publication Data

Hirschmann, Kris, 1967–
  Sharks / by Kris Hirschmann.
    p. cm. — (Nature's predators)
Includes bibliographical references (p.   ).
Summary: Describes the physical characteristics of sharks, their sensory systems, feeding habits, and some of the threats to their existence.
  ISBN 0-7377-1005-5 (hardback : alk. paper)
  1. Sharks—Juvenile literature. [1. Sharks.] I. Title. II. Series.
  QL638.9 .H57 2002
  597 .3—dc21

2001005161

Copyright 2002 by KidHaven Press,
an imprint of The Gale Group
10911 Technology Place, San Diego, CA 92127

No part of this book may be reproduced or used in any other form or by any other means, electrical, mechanical, or otherwise, including, but not limited to photocopy, recording, or any information storage and retrieval system, without prior written permission from the publisher.

Printed in the U.S.A.

Contents

Chapter 1: The Perfect Predator   5

Chapter 2: Incredible Senses   15

Chapter 3: Killing and Feeding   25

Chapter 4: Sharks in Danger   34

Glossary   43

For Further Exploration   45

Index   47

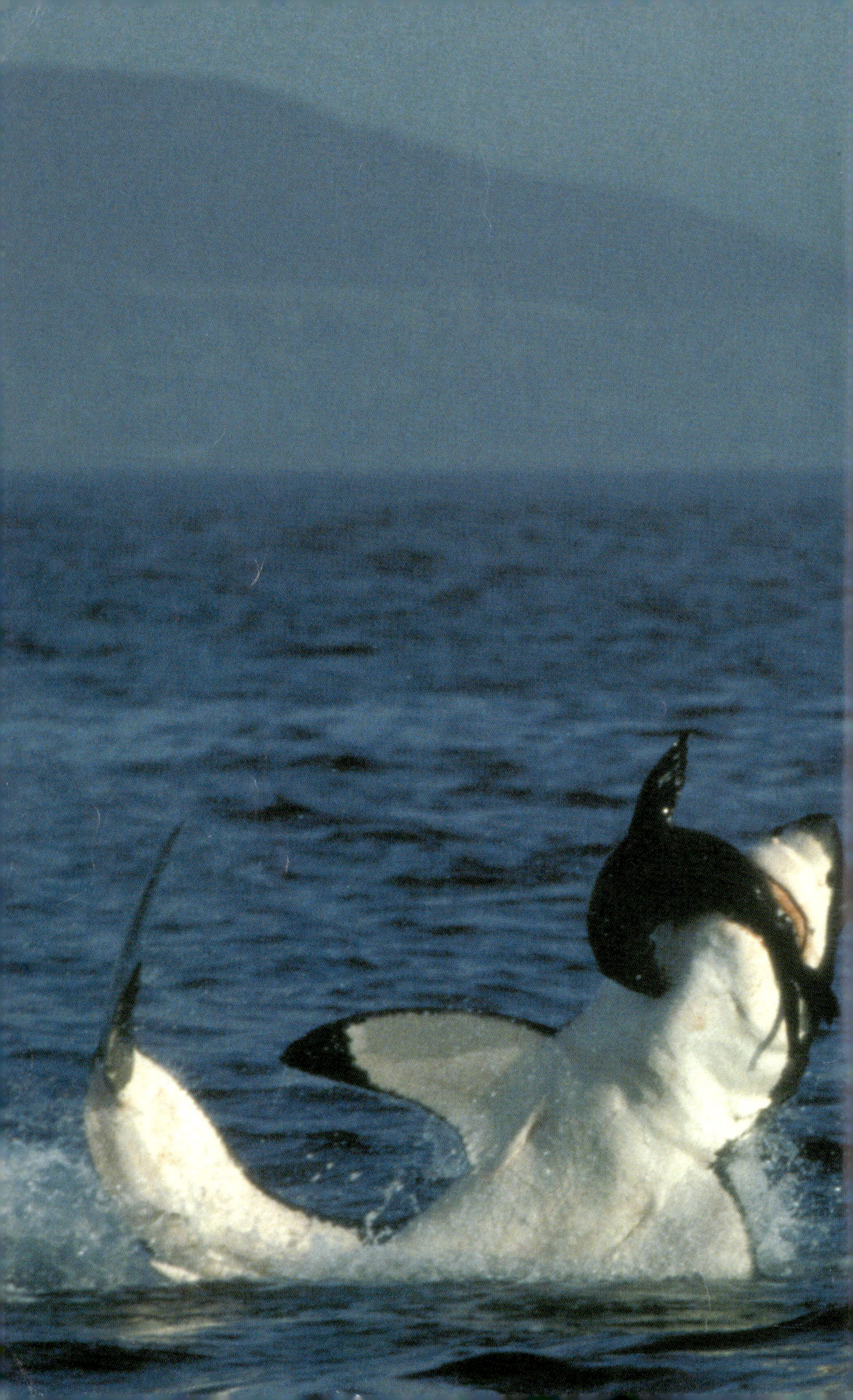

Chapter 1

The Perfect Predator

Sharks are a type of fish. They have sleek bodies that are perfectly designed to cut through ocean waters. They have keen senses that help them to get around and to find prey. And they have powerful muscles, sharp teeth, and other physical tools that make them efficient killers. Combined, these qualities make sharks the deadliest hunters in the seas.

Sharks have been swimming the earth's oceans for more than 400 million years. Fossil records show that their bodies have changed very little during this time. In shape and function, modern sharks are very similar to their ancestors. This is probably because sharks are such perfect **predators** that they have not had to change much to survive. Today's sharks have everything they need to rule the seas, just as their ancestors did millions of years ago.

Shark Basics

Scientists have identified about 460 different types, or species, of sharks. Some types of sharks are very common. Others are so rare that they have been spotted only a few times. And there are probably many types of sharks that have not yet been discovered.

Sharks can be found in every ocean in the world except the freezing Southern Ocean near Antarctica. The majority of sharks live in warm tropical and subtropical waters (the regions nearest the equator) where temperatures are greater than 70 degrees Fahrenheit. Some sharks prefer cooler waters, with temperatures ranging from 50 to 70 degrees Fahrenheit. And a very few sharks can be found swimming in the near-freezing waters of the Arctic Ocean, the North Atlantic, and the North Pacific.

Sharks can also be found in all different parts of an ocean. Some sharks live near land, while others spend their whole lives at sea. Some sharks cruise the sunny surface of the water, while others live thousands of feet deep. Some sharks swim constantly, while others are bottom dwellers that spend most of their time lying quietly on the ocean floor.

Sizes and Shapes

Sharks come in many different sizes. The world's biggest shark is the whale shark, which can measure 41 feet from nose to tail. The smallest shark is the dwarf shark, which is just 6 inches long. All other sharks lie somewhere between these two extremes, with most falling in the 3- to 10-foot range.

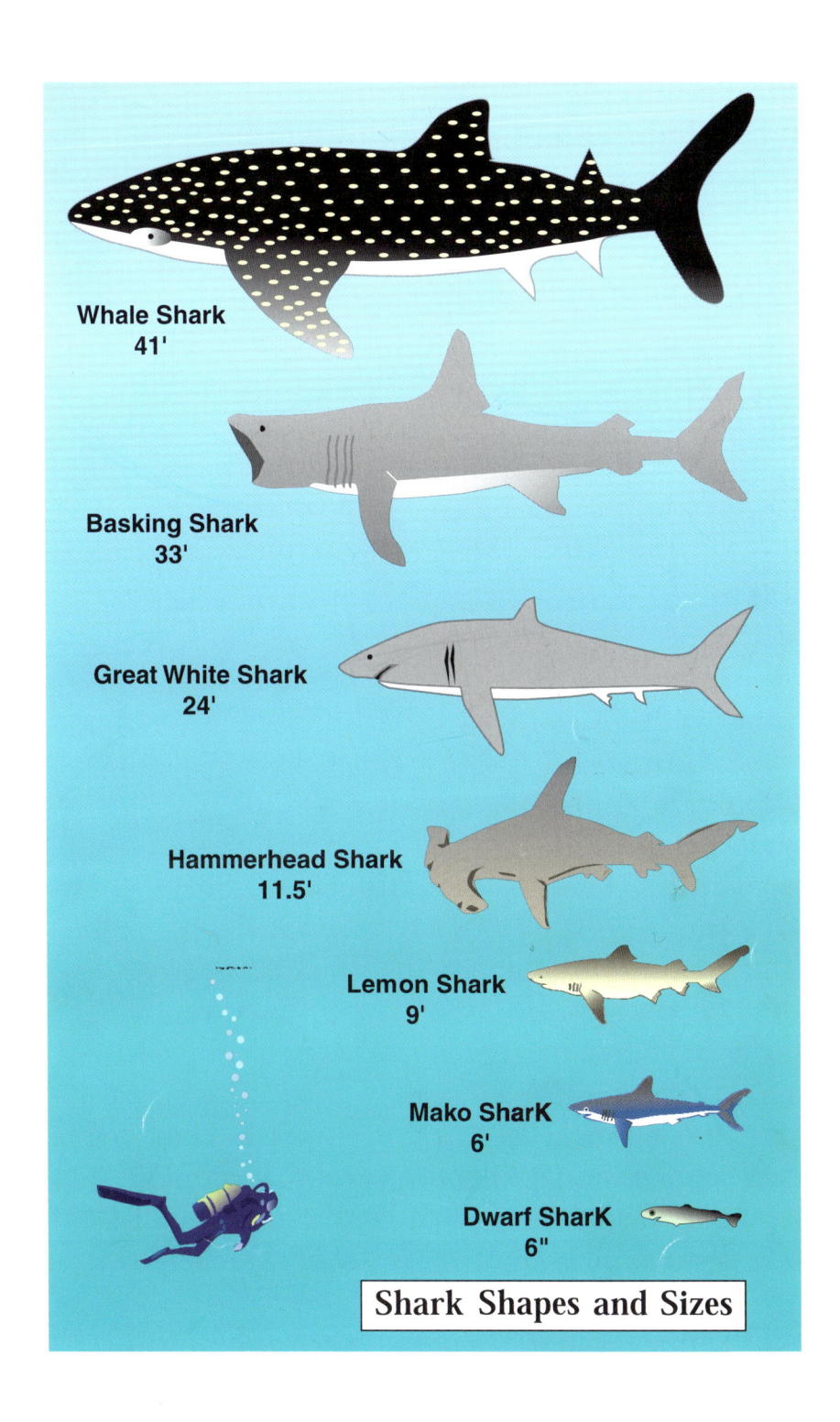

Whale Shark
41'

Basking Shark
33'

Great White Shark
24'

Hammerhead Shark
11.5'

Lemon Shark
9'

Mako SharK
6'

Dwarf SharK
6"

Shark Shapes and Sizes

7

Shark Features

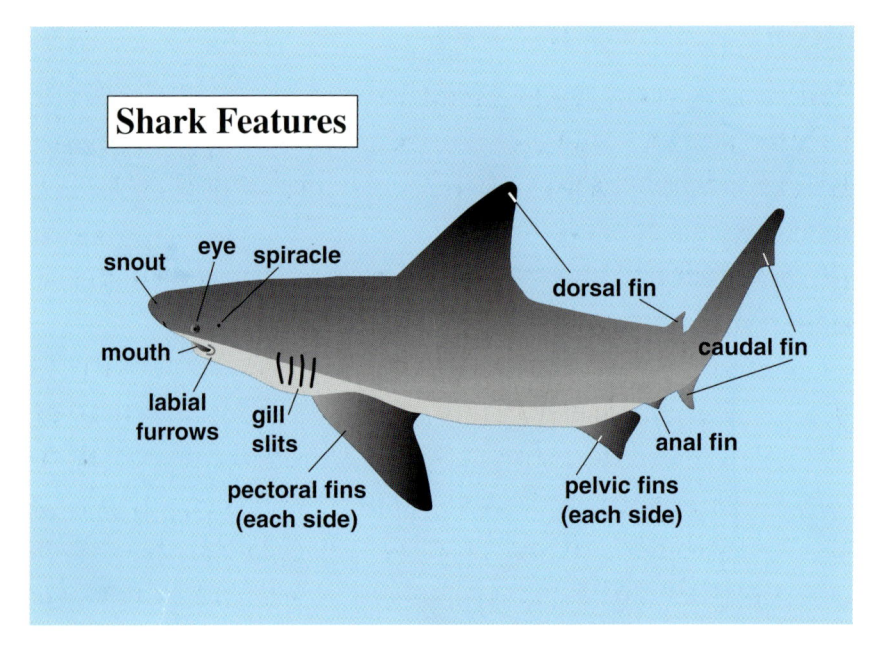

- snout
- eye
- spiracle
- mouth
- labial furrows
- gill slits
- pectoral fins (each side)
- dorsal fin
- caudal fin
- anal fin
- pelvic fins (each side)

Sharks also come in some unusual shapes. Some bottom-dwelling sharks, including angel sharks and sand devils, have flattened bodies. Others, including zebra sharks and catsharks, have long, flexible, snakelike tails. And some deep-water sharks, including the goblin shark and the megamouth shark, have flabby bodies that sag and droop near the ocean's surface.

But odd-shaped sharks are the exception. In terms of shape, most sharks share certain features: a firm, torpedo-shaped body; a triangular dorsal fin standing up from the back; pectoral fins just below and behind the gills; and a caudal fin bringing up the rear. These are not the only features that define a shark, but they are probably the best recognized. To prey, a glimpse of these features means that danger is approaching.

Streamlined Bodies

There is a good reason that most sharks are similar in shape. The typical shark body is very **streamlined**, which means that it creates little resistance, or **drag**, as it moves through the water. So a shark glides easily through the ocean, conserving precious energy that will be used later for hunting.

Sharks have another feature that decreases drag. Their skin is covered with tiny toothlike structures called **dermal denticles**. These denticles have ridges that channel water and make it flow smoothly around the shark's body. Denticles are usually covered by a slime that increases the streamlining effect even further.

The mako shark makes especially good use of its streamlined body. The mako cruises along at a gentle five to six miles per hour, looking for food as it goes. When the shark spots prey, it pushes its sleek body forward in a burst of speed. Makos

The mako shark's sleek body allows it to swim more than twenty miles an hour.

can travel at more than twenty miles per hour, which is faster than any other kind of shark.

Inside the Body

Sharks also have several features inside their bodies that help them to be efficient hunters. The most important internal feature is the skeleton, which is made of rubbery **cartilage** instead of bone. Cartilage is strong, but it is not as dense or as heavy as bone. So a shark's skeleton is both sturdy and lightweight.

Cartilage is also much more flexible than bone. Many sharks take full advantage of this flexibility when they hunt. A leopard shark, for instance, can twist its body into impossible-looking bends as it chases its prey. It blocks every escape attempt and soon catches its meal. Flexibility is very helpful to this amazing hunter.

A few sharks, including the mako and the great white, have another important internal feature. They can keep their bodies warmer than the surrounding water. A warm body functions better than a cold one, so these sharks have a big advantage over their colder and slower-moving prey.

Thousands of Teeth

A shark must kill its prey once it catches it. For this, the shark has a mouthful of teeth. The shape and size of the teeth depend on the shark's diet. Sharks that eat slippery prey such as fish and squid have small, needlelike teeth. Sharks that need to cut and tear the flesh of larger animals have triangular teeth with sharp, jagged edges like kitchen knives. And sharks that eat shellfish, crabs, and other tough prey have flat, slablike teeth that are good for crushing and grinding.

Sharks grow new teeth throughout their lives. At any time, a shark has one or more rows of fully grown, working teeth at the front of its mouth plus several rows of developing teeth farther inside. The developing teeth move forward in the mouth as they grow, similar to groceries on a conveyor belt. The old teeth drop out as the new ones reach the front. This process ensures that worn and broken teeth are quickly replaced by new and perfect ones. It also means that during

Shark Teeth

Lemon	Great White	Nurse
to grab & hold	to rip & tear	to crush & grind

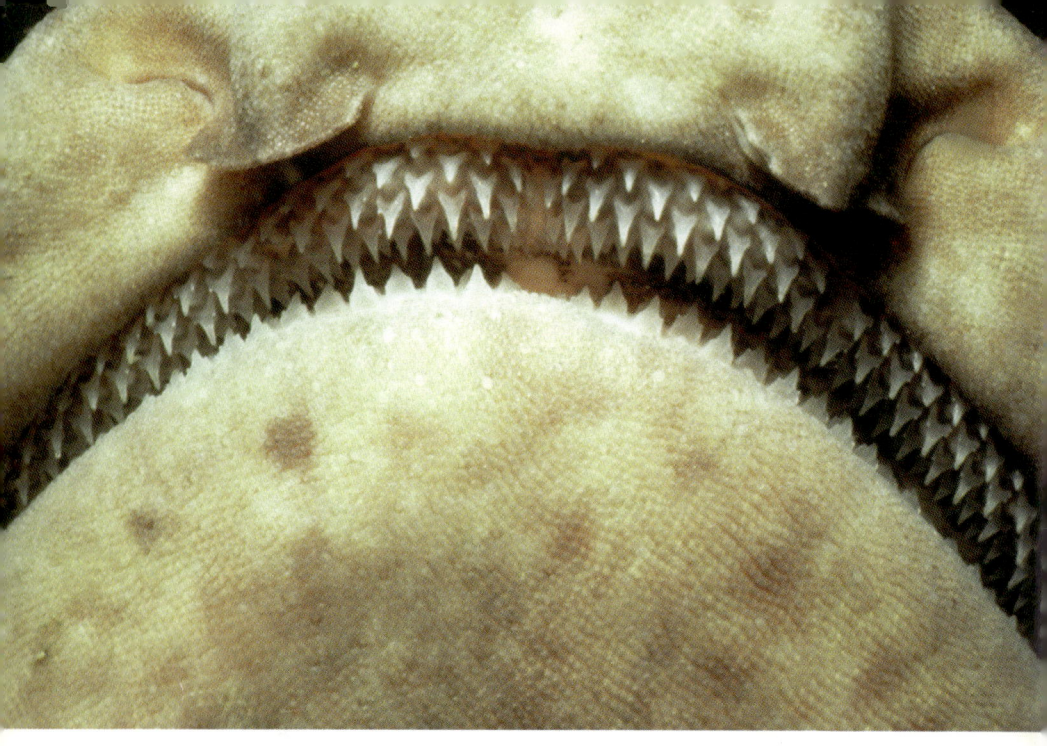

Shark teeth grow in several rows with working teeth in the front and developing teeth farther back in the mouth.

its lifetime, a shark goes through lots of teeth—sometimes as many as thirty thousand of them!

Strong, Flexible Jaws

A shark's mouth is positioned on the bottom of its body, well back from the snout. It looks as if it would be hard for a shark to bite its prey, but it is not, thanks to the shark's unique jaw structure. Both the upper and lower jaws are attached to the shark's skull by loose, stretchy ligaments and muscles. An attacking shark thrusts its jaws forward in its head, moving them into position for the bite.

The great white shark often uses this technique. As it moves toward prey, the great white raises its snout and pushes both of its jaws forward. This action makes the teeth of the bottom jaw point straight out at the prey. The shark uses these teeth to spear its prey. It then bites down with its powerful upper jaw to finish the job.

In addition to their flexible jaws, many sharks have incredible biting strength. The bite of a great white shark is more than twice as powerful as a lion's bite and more than fifteen times as powerful as a human's bite. Because their jaws are so strong, sharks can sometimes slice their victims in half with a single deadly chomp.

A great white shark lunges at a fisherman's bait, forcing its flexible jaws forward.

Perfect Predators

Between its jaws, its teeth, its strong body, and its other physical features, a shark is more than just a predator. It is one of nature's most perfect hunters. Few creatures are strong enough to fight off a hungry shark.

Chapter 2

Incredible Senses

All sharks are **carnivores**, which means they eat the flesh of other animals. As a group, sharks eat just about every living thing in the ocean. Fish, crab, lobster, eel, squid, and octopus are common meals for smaller sharks. Larger sharks will take bigger prey, including rays, turtles, floating sea birds, and other sharks. The biggest and strongest sharks can catch and kill large marine mammals such as seals, sea lions, dolphins, and whales. They may even eat humans if they get the chance.

A great white shark snatches a large seal on the water's surface.

Although most sharks will eat carrion (creatures that are already dead) if necessary, they prefer to kill their food themselves. But hunting comes before killing. A shark must track and catch its prey before it can settle in for a meal. This task is no problem for sharks, which have many amazing senses that are perfectly adapted to their hunting lifestyle.

Sounds Like Food

A shark usually hears prey long before it sees it. Sound travels more easily through water than through air, so sharks can hear noises made by prey from quite a long distance—sometimes as much as eight hundred feet.

A shark does not have external ears. Instead, it has two small openings on the top of its head.

The opening behind the eye of a shark leads to its inner ear.

The openings lead through canals to the shark's inner ears, which are full of tiny hairs. Sound vibrations enter the ear openings, pass through the canals, and eventually reach the inner ear, where they wiggle the hairs. These wiggling motions create electrical signals that travel to the shark's brain to be "heard" as sounds.

Like most predators, sharks prefer to hunt animals that are already wounded. Injured creatures are much easier for the shark to catch and kill. So sharks are attracted by sounds that are typical of struggling animals. Many of these sounds are so low that they cannot be heard by human ears. But a shark hears them clearly—and when it does, it usually goes looking for the source.

The Lateral Line

A wounded, thrashing fish does more than just make sounds. It also disturbs the water around it, sending a series of irregular waves outward in all directions. Sharks can "read" these waves with the help of a special organ called the **lateral line**.

The lateral line system consists mostly of two long, slender tubes, one running all the way down each side of a shark's body and onto the upper tail. Like the inner ears, these tubes are packed with tiny hairs. The hairs sway back and forth when water currents move past them, creating information that is sent to the shark's brain. The shark then uses this information to form a mental picture

Lateral Line

Skin surface

Interior of ear canal with moving hairs

Ear

Lateral Line

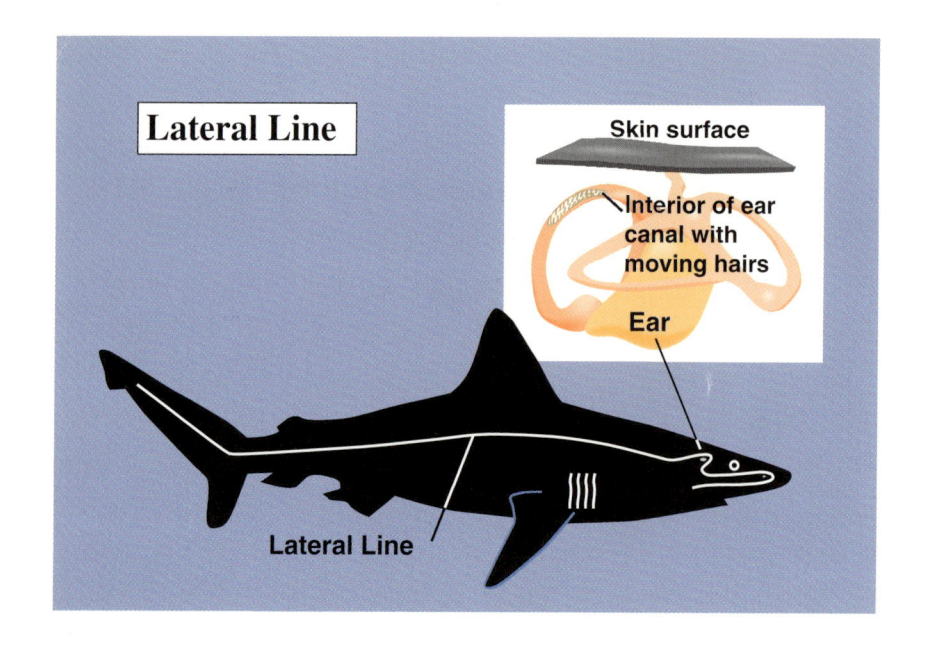

of its surroundings, including any prey that may be nearby.

The information created by the lateral line system is like hearing and touch rolled together into one super sense. Because it allows sharks to "feel" prey at a distance, even through cloudy water, this sense is very helpful to a hunting shark.

Following a Scent Trail

Sharks have another way of finding distant prey. They have an incredibly keen sense of smell. Smell is so important to sharks, in fact, that these animals devote about two-thirds of their brain to processing scent information.

Sharks do not smell a wide variety of things. They detect only the scents that are important to their survival—things such as the blood and bodily fluids of injured animals. Where these scents are concerned, a shark's sense of smell is amazingly sensitive. Experiments have shown that sharks can smell blood at concentrations of one part in 1 million. That is equal to about one pinhead-sized drop of blood dissolved in a full bathtub of water.

When a shark smells blood, it usually begins tracking the scent. The shark swings its head back and forth, bringing water into nasal sacs near the front of its snout and "sniffing" the water to see where the scent is strongest. The shark constantly corrects its direction so it is always swimming in the most concentrated part of

The scent of blood from bait attracts this shark to a diver's cage.

the scent stream. Before long, the shark will find the injured animal and perhaps a meal.

The distance at which a shark can smell blood depends mostly on the size of the prey. A shark needs to be quite close before it can smell the blood of a small fish. But a wounded seal or another large animal with lots of blood can attract sharks from a mile away or even more.

Shark Vision

A shark's senses of hearing, touch, and smell lead it to prey. But when the shark gets close enough, its vision takes over. "Close enough" depends on visual conditions. If the water is clear, a shark will begin hunting visually when it gets within about one hundred feet of its prey. If the water is cloudy, a shark may rely on its other senses until it is only a few feet from its meal.

A shark's eye structure depends on its environment. Sharks that live near the surface tend to have small eyes, while those that live in the dark depths of the ocean have enormous eyes that can catch even the tiniest glimmer of light.

Most sharks' eyes are located on the sides of their heads. This positioning gives sharks a wide field of vision but makes it hard for them to judge distance. Still, a shark gets plenty of information about its prey even without a good distance sense. Sharks can recognize the general outlines and colors of their usual prey. They can judge the prey's approximate location, and they can see where it is

Shark eyes come in many different shapes and sizes.

traveling and how fast it is moving. They can also decide whether an animal looks healthy and hard to catch, or whether it is wounded and therefore an easy target. A shark puts all of this information together before deciding whether to move in for the kill.

Electrical Senses

Sharks have an extra sense that helps them to hunt and to kill. Their snouts are covered with tiny pits that contain electricity-sensing organs called **ampullae of Lorenzini**. All living creatures give off weak electrical signals, and a shark uses its ampullae to detect these signals—and therefore its prey.

A shark must be very close to another animal before it can sense its electrical field, however. So a shark's electrosense is most useful during the actual attack. The shark uses the prey's electrical signals to guide its jaws to the target. At first, the signals may be fairly weak. But an injured animal gives off a stronger electrical field than a healthy one, so the prey's signals increase as the attack continues. The electrical surge excites the shark and encourages it to finish its deadly job.

Sharks may also use their electrical sense to find hidden prey. Hammerhead sharks are known for this behavior. A hammerhead often swims just above the ocean floor, swinging its broad, flat head back and forth like a metal detector. When it senses the electrical field of a

Ampullae of Lorenzini

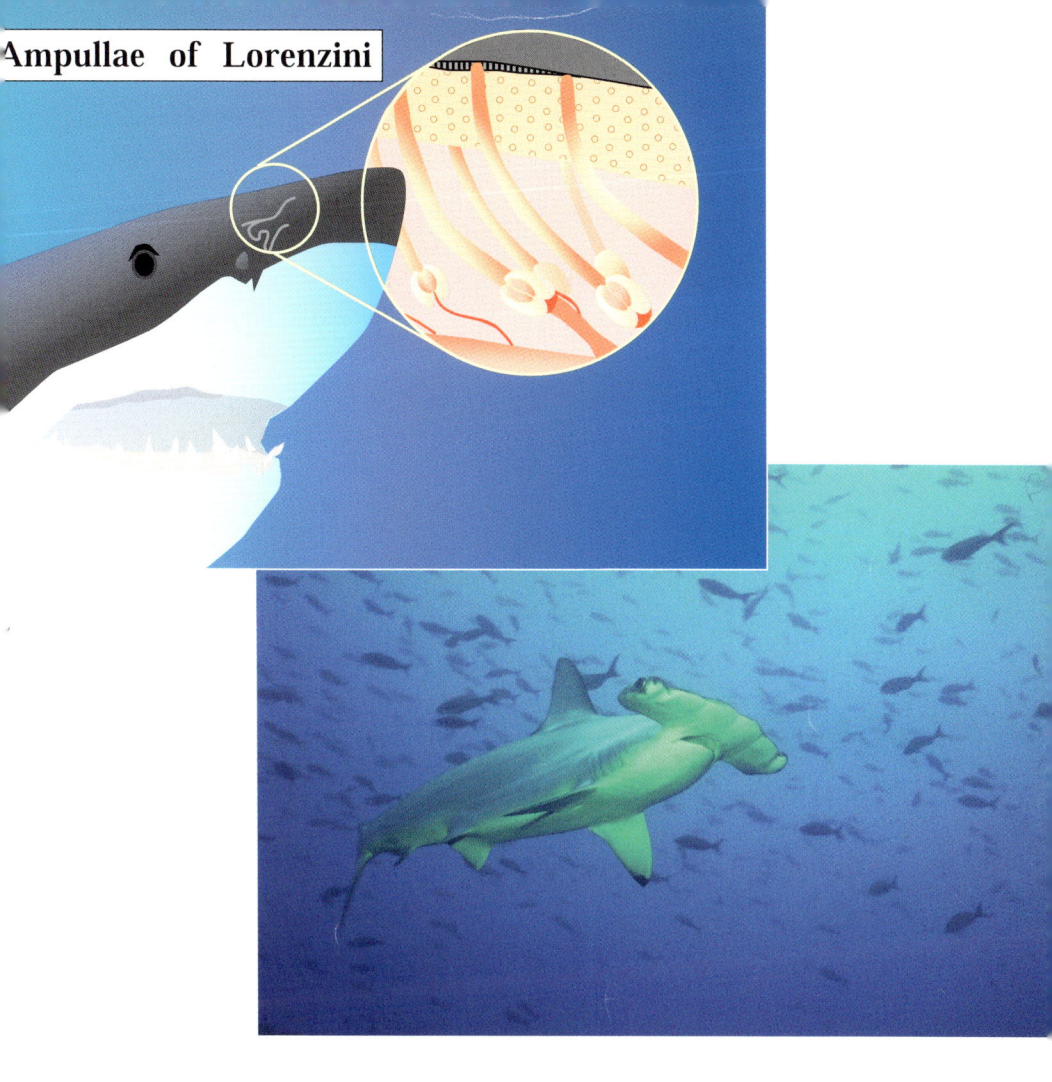

A hammerhead shark uses the electrical sensors in its head to find food on the ocean bottom.

buried stingray, the shark lunges downward and uses its head as a shovel to dig up its meal.

Many Techniques

Most sharks are active hunters, which means they chase their prey. Active hunters make good use of their amazing senses.

23

Shark Senses to Find Food

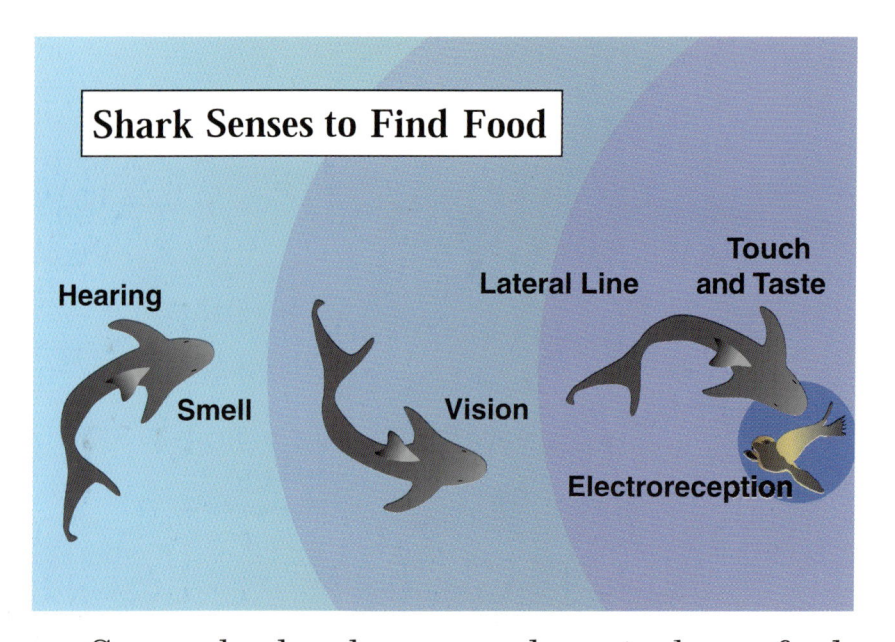

Hearing
Smell
Lateral Line
Vision
Touch and Taste
Electroreception

Some sharks, however, do not chase food. They let food come to them. Some sharks use the ambush technique, lying on the ocean floor and waiting for prey to approach. Other sharks are filter feeders. They swim along with their mouths hanging open, swallowing anything that happens to get swept down their throats. Because their hunting methods are passive, ambush and filter feeders do not depend as much on their super senses.

But no matter how they feed themselves, all sharks have one thing in common. They are perfectly equipped to catch the food they need to survive.

Chapter 3

Killing and Feeding

Between their powerful bodies and their incredible senses, sharks are hunting machines. To survive, sharks must eat, and they are very good at achieving that goal. A hungry shark *will* find prey—and when it does, it will kill and eat its prey with the same skill it applies to the hunt.

A seal is in grave danger as a great white shark breaches the water's surface.

Moving In for the Kill

When a shark locates prey, it approaches quickly and quietly, trying to avoid being seen until the last second. The shark's speed is very helpful in this task. So is its skin coloration. Most sharks are **countershaded**, which means they are dark on top and light on the bottom. Seen from below, the shark blends into the bright ocean surface. Seen from above, the shark disappears against the ocean floor. Between its coloring, its speed, and its silence, a shark can usually sneak up on prey without giving itself away.

A light belly and a dark back help sharks blend into their surroundings.

A shark attack often begins with a "test bite." A shark bites an animal gently, wounding it just a little bit and tasting its flesh and blood. If the animal tastes bad, the shark may abandon its attack. But if the shark likes what it tastes, it shifts into full killing mode. The shark rolls its eyes back in its head or covers them with a special membrane to protect them. Then it lunges at the prey, pushing its jaws forward as it moves. When the shark reaches the prey, it bites with all its strength.

Bite-Sized Chunks

A shark cannot chew. Instead, it gulps whatever food it can fit down its throat. If a prey animal is small, the shark may swallow it whole. If the prey is big, the shark will bite it over and over again, tearing off chunks that are small enough to eat.

A shark's bite may remove a perfect block of meat on the first try. But sometimes the prey is too big, or the bite does not do the job. When this happens a shark clamps its jaws tight, burying its teeth in the prey's body. The shark then shakes its head back and forth. This motion drives the teeth deeper and deeper into the prey. Before long the shark tears loose a bite-sized chunk of flesh.

This technique works especially well for sharks with serrated (jagged-edged) teeth. Tiger sharks, great whites, and other sharks with serrated teeth sometimes leave wounds so clean and

The carcass of a dead shark reveals both a clean bite (bottom) and a tearing bite (top).

smooth that they look like they were made with a sharp kitchen knife.

Group Feeding

Most sharks are solitary hunters. But a few types of sharks hunt cooperatively. Working together, a group of sharks can catch and kill prey that is much too big for one shark to handle on its own. Sevengill and great white sharks, for instance, sometimes gather in packs to kill large seals. And green dogfish, which are only ten inches long, prowl in large groups as they hunt for their favorite food—octopus. When they find an octopus they swarm all over it, tearing it apart with their sharp teeth.

Some sharks, including sand sharks, great whites, and threshers, may use a group hunting technique called **encircling**. Several sharks surround a school of fish, then circle closer and closer to herd the fish into a tight ball. When the fish are packed together, the sharks take turns swimming through the school and grabbing mouthfuls of food.

Sometimes many solitary sharks are attracted to the same food source. These sharks will all feed at the same time in the same place. But just because they are near each other does not mean they work together. Although the sharks are sharing food, each individual is looking out only for itself.

Feeding Frenzies

Group feeding is usually very controlled. Each shark eats its fill and ignores its neighbors. Under certain conditions, however, sharks feeding close to each other may become so excited that they start thrashing around and biting everything in sight, including the other sharks. This phenomenon is called a **feeding frenzy**.

A feeding frenzy gets its start when a large amount of food appears in an area. Many sharks show up and start to eat. As the injured animals bleed, the water begins to smell strongly of blood. This scent makes the sharks more and more aggressive. They twist their bodies back and forth in angry displays. They also begin to fight over the food, biting other sharks and sometimes hurting them badly or even killing them in the process. The sharks may get so worked up that they continue to attack each other even after the original food is gone.

Feeding frenzies are not common. They happen only in very unusual circumstances. It is likely that human fishing boats, which are often surrounded by dead and dying fish, cause most feeding frenzies.

Sharks aggressively fight for food during a feeding frenzy.

Big Appetites

Although sharks can be fierce, they also have a calmer side. Sharks are not always on the hunt. In fact, they often go days without eating. Most sharks eat once every two or three days.

A shark's eating patterns depend on its food requirements. Slow, sluggish sharks consume food equal to about 1 percent of their body weight per day. Fast, active sharks may consume up to 3 percent of their body weight per day. These numbers are averages, which means that the shark does not necessarily eat that amount every single day. It might eat several big meals one after the other, then wait a week or more before hunting again.

Most sharks stop hunting for a while after a big feed, giving themselves time to digest. But even a shark with a full belly will usually eat if an easy meal comes its way. Most sharks have loose, stretchy stomachs that can expand to hold a great deal of food. These big stomachs let sharks "stock up" when lots of prey is available. A shark that has stuffed itself with food can survive for many weeks without eating. Some sharks can even go months without a meal.

Amazing Hunters

Although all sharks are hunters, they do not all hunt in exactly the same way. Different sharks use different tricks and techniques, some of which are quite unusual. The thresher shark, for example, has a whiplike tail nearly as long as its body. The thresher uses its strong tail to bash its prey. Then it glides in and eats the stunned animals.

The great white shark is another shark that may immobilize its prey before eating it. A great white often bites seals and other large prey, then lets them go. The shark waits until the animal dies from its wounds before tracking it down and eating it.

The sixteen-inch-long cookie cutter shark does not worry about immobilizing prey. In fact, it does not even try to kill its prey. It simply takes a bite, then swims away. The cookie cutter feeds by pressing its mouthful of razor-sharp teeth against larger animals, then rotating its body and scooping out a two-inch plug of flesh. The cookie cutter's bite is seldom fatal, but it does leave a painful wound.

The ornate wobbegong shark has one of the easiest hunting techniques of all. It has a fleshy fringe around its mouth that it uses to lure prey. The wobbegong lies on the sea floor, wiggling its "tassels" so they look like worms. When a fish comes to investigate, the wobbegong opens its huge mouth and sucks the fish inside.

Unusual Diets

Other sharks hunt in the traditional manner but eat some unusual food. The bull shark, for exam-

The tiger shark is considered the garbage can of the sea.

ple, can live in freshwater. This makes it very dangerous to humans. The bull shark often enters rivers and lakes and occasionally attacks and eats people who are bathing or swimming near the shore.

The tiger shark may have the strangest diet of any shark. It is sometimes called the "garbage can of the sea" because it will eat anything. Items found in the stomachs of tiger sharks include lumps of coal, cans of paint, boat cushions, a horse's head, and human feet and arms.

Regardless of its diet, a shark is designed to kill—and to eat. Each shark has exactly the right tools to catch its chosen prey.

Chapter 4

Sharks in Danger

Many sharks, especially big ones, are **apex predators**. This means that they are at the top of their food chain. Apex predators eat many creatures, but no other animal depends on them as a food source.

But not all sharks are big enough to avoid being eaten. Smaller sharks often fall prey to other sea creatures, including other sharks. And even the largest sharks face plenty of dangers in their ocean home.

Hunting the Hunter

A shark's safety depends partly on its size. Most ocean predators stay away from the biggest sharks, preferring smaller and easier prey. But even the largest sharks are occasionally attacked. Killer whales (which range from fifteen to thirty feet in length) have been seen attacking great white sharks, and sperm whales (which can be more than sixty feet long) may also attack if they get the opportunity. Such attacks, however, are not common. The sheer size of a big shark usually discourages even the strongest predator.

Even the largest sharks sometimes become prey to ocean predators like this killer whale.

Small sharks are in much greater danger of being attacked. The attacks usually come from bigger and stronger sharks, but they sometimes come from other creatures, too. Killer whales and sperm whales are more likely to prey on small sharks than on big ones. Large groupers, some species of which may grow to thirteen feet in length and five hundred pounds in weight, have been seen feeding on reef sharks. And entire schools of dolphins and porpoises occasionally attack a shark, ramming it with their hard noses and sometimes even biting it. Dolphin and porpoise attacks, however, are not meant to kill the shark. They are meant to drive it away.

Pups Under Attack

Baby sharks (called pups) may be very small, measuring as little as 3½ inches in some species. Their size makes them vulnerable. Infant sharks make tasty meals for fish, wading birds, crocodiles, squid, bigger sharks, and other large creatures. A shark pup may even be eaten by its own mother.

In some shark species, including the sand tigers, makos, porbeagles, and threshers, the danger starts before birth. A female shark of these species initially carries as many as forty embryos (developing babies) in each of her two birth cham-

---

Predatory behavior in certain shark species begins as early as the embryo stage (seen here).

bers. When an embryo reaches a certain size, it starts eating its brothers and sisters. Only the strongest embryo in each chamber survives long enough to be born.

This process seems savage, but it has a purpose. The ocean world is a harsh one where only the toughest animals are successful. Cannibalism before birth ensures that only the strongest sharks survive to see the light of day.

Shark Defenses

When a shark comes under attack, it defends itself with the same weapons it uses on the hunt. A shark's powerful body and sharp teeth are enough to discourage most would-be attackers.

A few sharks, however, have some extra defenses that help to keep them safe. The bramble shark and the prickly dogfish, for instance, have sharp spines all over their bodies. Other sharks, including the gulper shark and the hornshark, have two spikes on their backs that give painful pokes to biting predators. Eating a spiky shark is very uncomfortable, so a predator that bites one of these creatures does not usually return for a second helping.

Some sharks defend themselves with protective skin coloration called **camouflage**. This is the main strategy for sluggish sharks such as the angel shark and the wobbegong. By making it hard for predators to see them, these sharks stay out of trouble with very little effort.

The spike of the horn shark (top) and the skin color of the wobbegong (bottom) help these sharks repel attackers.

The swellshark has an especially useful defense. When threatened, it swims into narrow gaps between rocks, then gulps so much water that its stomach inflates to three times its normal size. The swollen shark is wedged so tightly between the rocks that no predator can tear it loose.

The Fear Factor

A shark's defenses work well against its natural ocean-dwelling enemies. They do not work so well against people, who kill millions of sharks every year.

Fear plays a big role in the relationship between humans and sharks. The world's human population has grown larger and larger over the past century, which means that more and more humans live, work, and play near oceans. As a result, the chance of shark attacks on humans has increased. The number of actual attacks is still small: During the year 2000, for instance, the scientific community's International Shark Attack File recorded seventy-nine unprovoked shark attacks on humans. (Between January and September 2001, fifty-two shark attacks were reported worldwide.) These totals are tiny compared to the number of sharks and swimmers that share the ocean each year. But many people are terrified of sharks anyway.

Because of this fear, some governments have encouraged their citizens to kill certain types of sharks. These policies have caused the deaths of thousands of sharks. So have antishark nets,

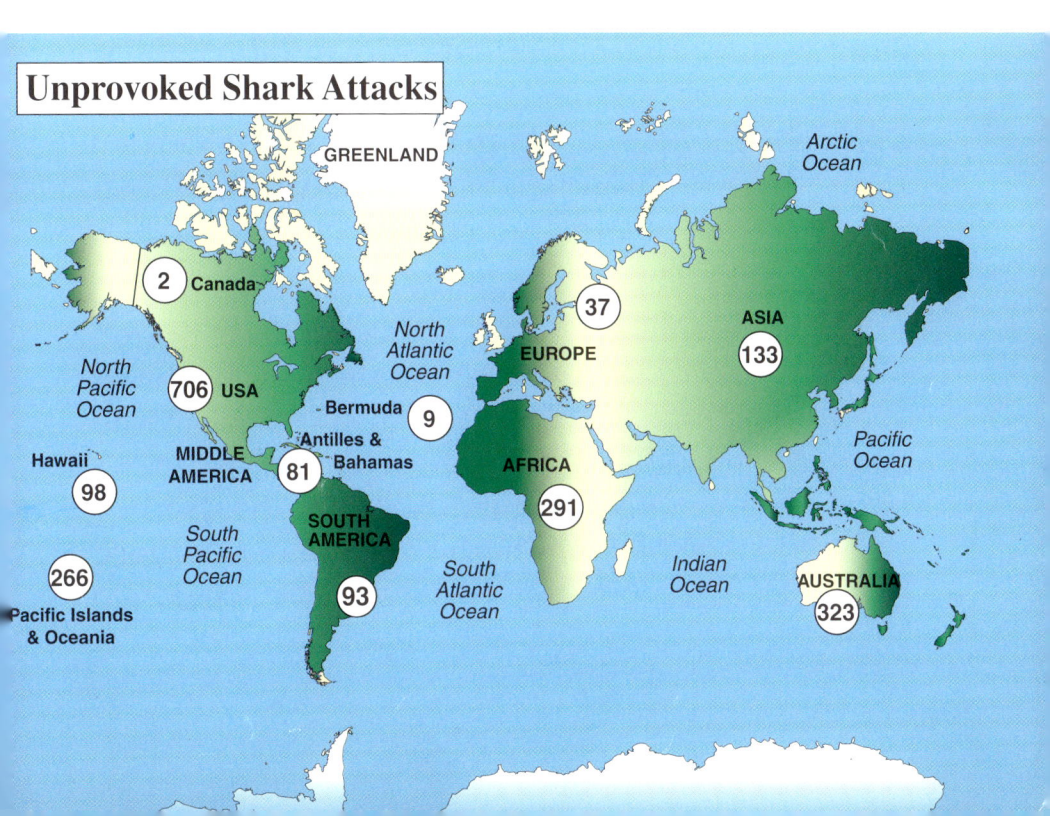

Unprovoked Shark Attacks

Region	Attacks
Canada	2
USA	706
Hawaii	98
Pacific Islands & Oceania	266
Middle America	81
Antilles & Bahamas (Bermuda)	9
South America	93
Europe	37
Africa	291
Asia	133
Australia	323

A shark carcass is tangled in an antishark net.

which are fine meshes surrounding public beaches. The nets protect swimmers but they are deadly to sharks, which often get tangled up in the mesh and suffocate or starve to death.

Sharks for Sale

Sharks are also killed for their commercial uses. There is a worldwide market for shark flesh, which is a popular food in many areas. Shark fins are in great demand in the Orient as a soup ingredient. Shark cartilage is used in some vitamin supplements, shark oil is used to make cosmetics, and even sharkskin has its uses: A shark's rough hide makes good sandpaper, and it may also be cured and made into boots, belts, and other leather products.

Commercial fisheries are responding to the human demand for shark products by hauling millions of sharks out of the ocean each year. This technique may be acceptable (when regulated) for fish that reproduce quickly and constantly rebuild their populations. But it is very damaging to the world shark population. Sharks reproduce much more slowly than most fish, which means they cannot bounce back like other species do. Commercial fishing is therefore a great threat to sharks around the world.

Even boats that target tuna, swordfish, and other bony fish are a danger to sharks. These boats catch many millions of sharks by accident

Dozens of shark fins, prized in the Orient for their flavor.

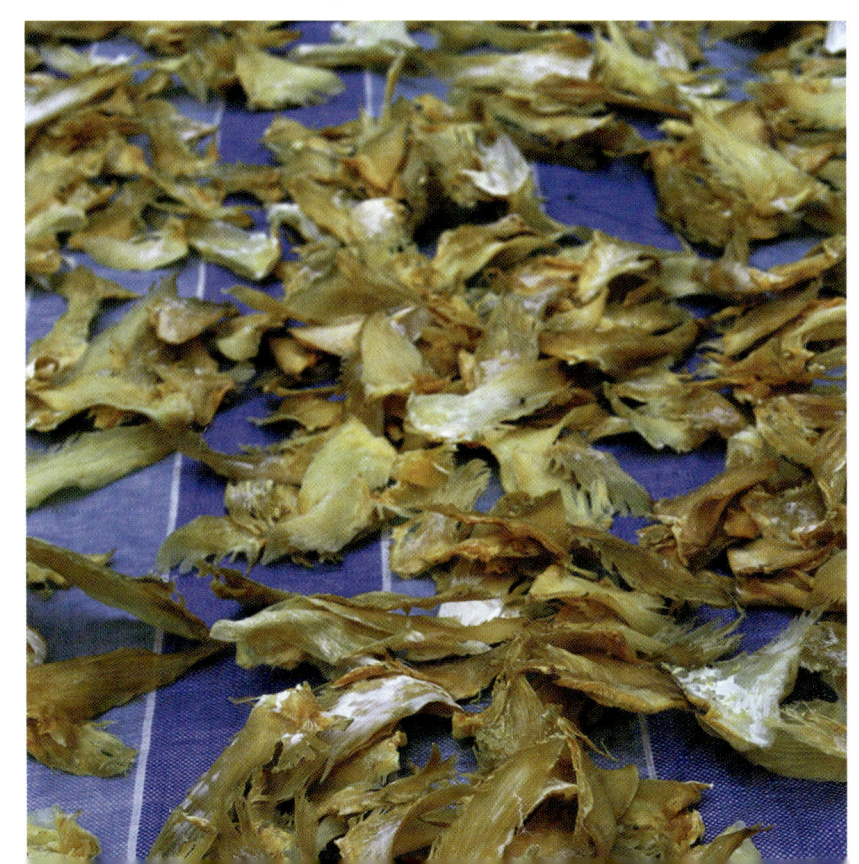

every year. Sharks taken accidentally are called **bycatch**, and usually they are not kept. Their dead bodies are tossed back into the ocean to rot.

The Outlook for Sharks

Commercial shark fishing and bycatch problems have seriously hurt the shark populations in many areas, to the point that some species are in danger of extinction. Regulations and laws could protect sharks. However, such regulations sometimes make it hard for fisheries to catch other species. For this reason, many governments do not want to put shark protection laws in place. A few countries have passed such laws, but most have not.

Public education may be the answer. Many people see sharks as dangerous and frightening, and they do not really care what happens to them. Conservation groups around the world are working to change that view. They hope to make people understand that sharks are beautiful and fascinating creatures with an important role in the ocean ecosystem. Like any predator, sharks are a necessary part of the food chain—and without them, nature becomes unbalanced.

When people understand sharks' role, they may be more willing to support conservation efforts. And with the human threat reduced, there is hope that these magnificent hunters will continue to rule the seas as they have already done for millions of years.

Glossary

ampullae of Lorenzini: Organs that sense electrical fields, including the weak signals given off by all living creatures.

apex predator: A predator that is at the top of its food chain.

bycatch: Creatures caught by accident while hunting for something else.

camouflage: Skin coloration that matches the shark's surroundings.

carnivore: Any animal that eats only the flesh of other animals.

cartilage: The rubbery material from which shark skeletons are made.

countershading: Body coloration that is darker on top and lighter on the bottom.

dermal denticles: Tiny toothlike structures that cover a shark's skin.

drag: A force that tends to slow a body moving through a fluid.

encircling: A hunting technique in which several sharks surround a school of fish.

feeding frenzy: A group feeding situation in which many sharks gather, then become overexcited and extremely aggressive.

lateral line: An organ that detects and interprets disturbances in the water.

predator: Any animal that hunts other animals to survive.

streamlined: Shaped in a way that reduces resistance when moving through a fluid.

For Further Exploration

Books

Caroline Arnold, *Giant Shark: Megalodon, Prehistoric Super Predator*. New York: Clarion Books, 2000. Read about the extinct megalodon, the biggest shark ever to swim the earth's seas.

Dana Del Prado, *Terror Below! True Shark Stories*. New York: Grosset & Dunlap, 1997. A California surfer, a pearl diver, and a spear-fishing champion fight for their lives in three amazing-but-true stories.

Keith Elliot Greenberg, *Marine Biologist: Swimming with the Sharks*. Woodbridge, CT: Blackbirch Press, 1996. A real-life marine biologist takes readers on a tour of his shark research facility on the island of Bimini.

Amanda Harman, *Endangered! Sharks*. Tarrytown, NY: Benchmark Books, 1996. This book introduces readers to three threatened shark species: great whites, whale sharks, and basking sharks.

Marie Levine, *Great White Sharks*. Austin, TX: Raintree Steck-Vaughn, 1998. An in-depth look at the life of one of the world's most dangerous predators.

Christopher Maynard, *Informania: Sharks*. Cambridge, MA: Candlewick Press, 1997. A dynamic layout makes this book fun to read as well as informative.

Websites

Island of the Sharks (www.pbs.org/wgbh/nova/sharks). This site has lots of great pictures plus information on sharks' bodies, habits, and habitats. It also features an "Ask the Experts" section.

Shark Surfari! (www.nationalgeographic.com/features/97/sharks/index.html). An interactive online quiz about sharks. Test your knowledge!

Shark Tank (www.discovery.com/area/nature/sharks/tank.html). This site has in-depth information about some of the best-known sharks, including great whites, hammerheads, and more. Includes video clips.

Zoom Sharks (www.enchantedlearning.com/subjects/sharks/index.html). A good general information site. Includes information sheets on some well-known sharks plus black-and-white shark pictures to print out and color.

Index

ampullae of Lorenzini, 22–23
angel sharks, 8, 37

baby sharks. *See* pups
birds, 15
blood, 19
body temperature, 10
bramble sharks, 37
bull sharks, 32–33
bycatch, 42

camouflage, 26, 37
carrion, 16
cartilage, 10, 40
catsharks, 8
conservation, 42
cookie cutter sharks, 32
countershading, 26

defenses, 37–38
dermal denticles, 9
diet, 10–11
dogfish, 37
dolphins, 35
drag, 9
dwarf sharks, 6

eating
  biting and, 27
  feeding frenzies and, 29–30
  patterns of, 31
education, 42
electrical senses, 22–23
embryos, 36–37
extinction, 42

eyes, 20, 22, 27

feeding frenzies, 29–30
fins, 8, 40
fish, 11, 15, 32
fishing, 41–42
flexibility, 10, 12–13
fossils, 5

"garbage can of the sea," 33
goblin sharks, 8
great white sharks
  body temperature of, 10
  hunting techniques of, 13, 28, 29, 32
  as prey, 34
  teeth of, 27–28
green dogfish, 28
groupers, 35
gulper sharks, 37

habitats, 6, 8, 32–33
hammerhead sharks, 22–23
hearing, sense of, 16–17
hornsharks, 37
humans
  attacks on, 15, 33, 38–39
  as predators, 39–41
hunting
  ambush technique, 24
  cooperative, 28
  electrical senses and, 22–23
  encircling and, 29
  filter feeders and, 23
  flexibility and, 10
  immobilization of prey and, 32

47

jaws and, 12–13
lateral line system and, 17–18
passive techniques of, 23, 32
scent and, 18–20
sound and, 16–17
speed and, 26
tails and, 32
test bites and, 27
wounding of prey and, 32

International Shark Attack File, 39

jaws, 12–13, 27

killer whales, 34, 35

lateral line system, 17–18
leopard sharks, 10

mako sharks
  body temperature of, 10
  as embryos, 36–37
  speed of, 9–10
mammals, marine, 15, 35
megamouth sharks, 8

nets, 39–40

octopus, 28
oil, 40

porbeagles, 36–37
porpoises, 35
prey
  carrion as, 16
  cooperative hunting of, 28
  injured, 17, 22
  sharks as, 15, 34–37, 39–41
  size and, 15–16
  teeth and, 10–11
pups, 36

rays, 15, 22–23
reef sharks, 35

sand devils, 8
sand sharks, 29, 36
seals, 28, 32
sevengill sharks, 28
sharks
  as apex predator, 24
  as bycatch, 42
  as filter feeders, 24
  as prey, 15, 39–41
    embryos, 36–37
    pups, 36
  size and, 34–35
  shape of, 8–9
  sizes of, 6
  species of, 5
  see also specific types of sharks
shellfish, 12, 15
sight, sense of, 20, 22
skeletons, 10
skin
  coloration of, 26, 37
  commercial uses of, 40
  denticles on, 9
smell, sense of, 18–20
speed, 9–10, 26
sperm whales, 34, 35
squid, 12
stingrays, 22–23
stomachs, 31
swellsharks, 38

teeth
  as defense, 37
  diet and, 10–12
  serrated, 27–28
test bites, 27
threshers, 36–37
tiger sharks, 27–28, 33
turtles, 15

whales, 34, 35
whale sharks, 6
wobbegong sharks
  hunting techniques of, 32
  skin coloration of, 37

zebra sharks, 8

48

ST. EDMUND SCHOOL LIBRARY
11212 - 130 AVENUE, EDMONTON